World's Greatest
SPORTS STARS

Wonder House

(An imprint of Prakash Books)

Wonder House

(An imprint of Prakash Books)

contact@wonderhousebooks.com

ISBN : 9789388810364

CONTENTS

CRISTIANO RONALDO

BIRTH: *February 5, 1985*
Funchal, Portugal

Cristiano Ronaldo is a Portuguese soccer athlete who is one of the greatest football players of his generation.

Cristiano Ronaldo was born on February 5, 1985, in Madeira, Portugal, to José Dinis Aveiro and Maria Dolores dos Santos. His father named him Ronaldo after his favorite actor, Ronald Reagan, who was then the US president. Ronaldo has one older brother, Hugo, and two elder sisters, Elma and Liliana Cátia. Growing up, his family's financial condition was unstable, due to the fact that his father was an alcoholic. Ronaldo lost his father to kidney problems in 2005.

Ronaldo took an interest in football from a very young age. His father used to be a manager at the local amateur football club, thus, at the age of eight, Ronaldo began to play football. At the age of ten, he signed a contract with the local club, Clube Desportivo Nacional. In 1997, he joined one of the biggest clubs in Portugal, called Sporting Clube de Portugal.

In 2002, he made his debut with Sporting Lisbon's team. Ronaldo was the only player who played for all levels: under-16, under-17, under-18 and B-team. And after he graduated, he was added to the senior team in 2002.

At the age of seventeen, Ronaldo played his first game for Sporting Lisbon in the Portuguese Super League. Due to his great performance against Manchester United, the English club signed the young man for more than twelve million pounds. He scored the first three goals in the league and also helped his club to win the championship in the 2004 FA Cup final. He became the top athlete in his club and signed a five-year contract with Manchester United. During those five years, Ronaldo helped his club to win three premier league titles.

The Manchester United Football Club was the stepping stone for Ronaldo. He is known as the first-ever Portuguese player of the English club. On Sir Alex Ferguson's insistence, he wore the famous number 7 shirt. Ferguson had complete faith in his talent, stating, "We've had some fantastic number sevens, Bryan Robson, Eric Cantona, David Beckham, some wouldn't want that jersey but his [Ronaldo's] confidence was high even at 18. When he made his debut as substitute against Bolton he took the place by storm." Ronaldo became one of the best players in the world, scoring 84 goals in 196 league games for the club.

In 2009, Ronaldo became the most expensive player in the world. After Spain's Real Madrid paid a whopping $131 million to Manchester United, Ronaldo left the club and joined the new team. Till date, Ronaldo has broken many records for Real Madrid, since 2009. He scored forty goals during La Liga 2010-11, the highest number of goals till that year. In the following season he helped his team bag the La Liga championship by scoring a personal-best of 46 goals.

Ronaldo started his international career very early on. He was selected in the under-15 Portugal team. In 2003, Ronaldo first appeared in Portugal's national team when he played against Kazakhstan. He became the captain of the national team in 2008 and played three World Cups for Portugal. In the 2018 World Cup, Ronaldo performed exceptionally and scored four goals in four games.

Ronaldo is one of the highest paid athletes in sports history with brand endorsements such as Nike under his belt. He even released his own brand of products, like shoes and fragrances, called CR7.

Ronaldo has used his wealth for a lot of charitable causes. When a tsunami hit Southeast Asia, in 2004, he sought to help the victims. He auctioned a number of his things and raised funds for charity. He took part in the campaign against Ebola with other footballers. He also donated $8 million to help earthquake victims in Nepal. His most recent project was to fund the construction of a pediatric hospital in Santiago, Chile. He wishes to get involved in more charity projects in the future.

Ronaldo is currently in a relationship with Georgina Rodriguez, with whom he has three children.

DAVID BECKHAM

BIRTH: May 2, 1975
Leytonstone, England

Ðavid Beckham is a former football player from England. He is best known for playing as a mid-fielder for Manchester United and Real Madrid in his prime years. He is the master of free kicks.

David Beckham's full name is David Robert Joseph Beckham. He was born on May 2, 1975 in London, England to Ted Beckham and Sandra Georgina.

David's love for football started because of his

parents who were die-hard fans of Manchester United. As a kid, he used to spend his time playing football and dreamed of becoming a footballer. He used to play for a local football team called the Ridgeway Rovers.

For his early education, David went to Chase Lane Primary School and then attended Chingford County High School. He participated in many sports in school, but his focus mainly remained on becoming a footballer. David gave many trials at football clubs like Norwich City and Leyton Orient before he was selected by Tottenham Hotspur. At the age of eleven, he won the Bobby Charlton Soccer Schools National Skills Competition. David was only sixteen when he was selected to play for Manchester United's training division.

Two years later, he was officially a part of the club and by 1995 he was playing full-time. Beckham was a big part of Manchester United's wins in the Premier League, especially in achieving a treble in the league.

Beckham is best known for his stint with

Manchester United. He played with the team for eight seasons and led them to new heights. In 1999, he played in three major tournaments and led Manchester United to victory. These were the Premier League, the FA Cup and the UEFA Champions League.

Beckham has won six Premier League medals. The year 1998 was a slightly shaky one for Beckham while he played for England in the World Cup. England was removed from the tournament due to penalties in round sixteen. The team was criticized by both fans and the media. The same continued in the UEFA European Championship of 2000, as England was eliminated in the first round. Beckham became the team captain of the English national team in 2000. He scored the last goal in a World Cup qualifier against Greece, sending the team into the main tournament. Beckham has scored 17 goals for England.

In 2003, Beckham changed teams, from Manchester United to Real Madrid, and played for them for the next four years. He scored thirteen goals in that duration. He was considered to be a

Galactico, a term used for Real Madrid stalwarts including the likes of Ronaldo, Luis Figo and Roberto Carlos.

In 2007, he moved to the American team LA Galaxy and played with them for five years. It was a major move in Beckham's career. However, after he moved to the United States, he started to get injured frequently. He sprained his knee ligament in the first season and later had a tendon injury due to which he couldn't participate in the 2010 World Cup.

In 2013, he joined Paris Saint-Germain, and helped them win the French Ligue 1 title. He signed a 5-month contract with the team and donated all the money to charity. In 2013, Beckham announced his retirement after having played for 21 years.

Apart from his football career, he is also known as a style icon and has done many commercials. In 1998, he earned $13 million in endorsements alone. In 2003, he signed a $160 million lifetime contract with Adidas. He had a ten-year long collaboration with Pepsi Co. (till 2009) and has done promotions for Disney's theme parks.

David's personal life also led him to branching out into other professions. He married the former Spice Girls band member, Victoria Adams on July 4, 1999. The couple has four children. Beckham and his wife have worked as spokespersons for clothing designers, health and fitness specialists, fashion magazines, perfume and cosmetics manufacturers and hair stylists.

Beckham regularly donates a big part of his income to charitable causes. He is a Goodwill Ambassador for UNICEF's Sports Development program. In 2009, he founded the Malaria No More UK Leadership Council. He launched 7: The David Beckham UNICEF Fund to protect vulnerable children.

DIEGO MARADONA

BIRTH: *October 30, 1960*
Lanús, Argentina

Diego Maradona is a former Argentinean football player and is considered to be one of the greatest football players of all time. Diego helped his teams become champions in Argentina, Italy, and Spain. He was part of the Argentinean national team that won the 1986 World Cup.

Diego Armando Maradona was born on October 30, 1960, in Lanús, Argentina to Diego

Sr. and Dalma Salvadora Franco. He grew up in a low-income family and suffered financially. He was gifted a soccer ball at the age of three and he took an immediate interest in the game. When Maradona was eight, he caught the attention of a talent scout while he played in a local football club called Estrella Roja. The scout immediately selected the young Maradona for the youth team of Buenos Aires' Argentinos Juniors. He became the leading player on their team named Las Cebollitas (The Little Onions), one of the biggest junior clubs in Argentina, at the age of ten.

Maradona got his first big break at the age of fourteen. In 1976, he started playing with Argentinos Juniors itself, at the age of 14. And just four months later, he also joined the junior national team, becoming the youngest player to do so. He played for five years in the club. While there, he scored 115 goals in 167 games before moving to the Boca Juniors. He was signed on for $1 million in 1981. Diego managed to uplift his family from poverty on the basis of this contract. The same year, he contributed to the success of his club when he won them the League

Championship. After the League's success, Maradona was selected for the Argentinean senior national team. Getting the opportunity to play in the 1982 World Cup was a career high for Maradona. However, his team didn't do as well as expected.

Maradona transferred to Spain's FC Barcelona after his failure at the World Cup. He signed a $5 million contract, a record-setting fee at the time. He proved quite beneficial for the team. In 1983, Maradona led the team to winning the Copa del Rey and Spanish Super Cup. In just two years, he had scored 38 goals in 58 matches. But Maradona suffered quite a bit while he was in Barcelona. He fell ill and sustained multiple injuries. It took him three months to recover fully. After his recovery, he decided to transfer to an Italian team called SSC Napoli in 1984.

Maradona performed incredibly well during his time in Napoli. He even grabbed the media's attention. During 1986–87 and 1989–90 he directed the team for two seasons and won the Serie A Italian championships twice.

In 1986, Maradona led the Argentinean team to victory at the FIFA World Cup. He scored two of the most remarkable goals in World Cup history during a quarter-final against England. His second goal in the quarterfinals was voted as the 'Goal of the Century' by FIFA.com users. He was also awarded the Golden Ball Award for being the top scorer. Apart from the World Cup, he was also on the winning team, SSC Napoli, of the Coppa Italia in 1987 and the UEFA Cup in 1989.

In 1990, Maradona once again became the Argentinean captain for the 1990 FIFA World Cup. However, they did not win the trophy this time around and could only reach the finals. In 1992, Maradona left Napoli to join the Spanish team, Sevilla FC, for a year. Maradona also participated in the 1994 FIFA World Cup but was disqualified for testing positive for the drug Ephedrine. After a prosperous seventeen-year-long career, Maradona declared his retirement in 1997.

In the years after his retirement, he suffered from a lot of health issues. He was hospitalized a couple of times due to heart problems. He also had to undergo surgery to curb his obesity. Being a former football star, Maradona started training other players. In 2008, he became the head coach of the Argentinean national team till after the 2010 World Cup, where they lost a quarter-final against Germany.

Maradona married Claudia Villafane on November 7, 1984. But the marriage didn't last and the couple divorced in 2004. Maradona is the father of two daughters that he had with Villafane.

SIR DONALD BRADMAN

BIRTH: August 27, 1908
Cootamundra, Australia

DEATH: February 25, 2001 (aged 92)
Adelaide, Australia

Sir Donald Bradman was an Australian cricketer, commonly referred to as "The Don". He had a test batting average of 99.94. This has been even called as the greatest achievement by a sportsman in any major sport. In 1997, John Howard, Prime Minister of Australia, called him 'the greatest living Australian'.

Bradman was born to George and Emily Bradman on August 27, 1908 in New South Wales, Australia. Bradman played cricket from a very early age. As a child, Bradman worked on his timing by hitting a golf ball against a water tank. Bradman scored his first century when he was merely twelve years old, while playing for his high school.

Bradman made his debut when he was nineteen years old at the Adelaide Oval. He scored 118 runs for the New South Wales cricket team. In 1928, the cricketer played his first test match against England. His debut performance was not noteworthy, but he scored 79 and 112 runs in the third test match at the Melbourne Cricket Ground. Bradman became the youngest player at the time to have scored a test century.

In 1930, he was chosen to play in the Ashes series against England. He scored 131 and 254 runs in the first and the second tests respectively. In the third test match, he recorded a triple century, and scored a double century in the fourth and final match, thus, contributing to

Australia's win in the Ashes.

The 1932-33 Ashes series was held in Australia. The English player, Douglas Jardine, came up with the 'bodyline' tactic to combat the batting skills of Bradman. This bowling tactic was considered to be physically threatening for a batsman. This affected Bradman's performance in the match. His batting average of the series was 56. England won the series.

In the 1938 tour of England, the cricketer performed exceedingly well. Bradman played in 26 innings and scored 13 centuries for his team. During the Second World War, in 1940, the cricketer joined the Royal Australian Air Force on aircrew duty. However, he soon got transferred to the army as a lieutenant. Bradman was posted at the Army School of Physical Training. His health was severely affected during his time there, due to the stressful job. In 1941, he was discharged from service.

In the mid-1940s, Bradman returned to cricket. He played his final test match at The Oval in 1948, against England. The cricketer ended his career with a test batting average of 99.94. Bradman is the only test player to have scored 300 runs in a single day.

Donald Bradman scored 6996 runs in 52 test matches throughout his career. He has scored a total of 29 international test centuries. He held the record of scoring 974 runs in a series, the most scored by any player in test history till date. In 1949, he was knighted for his services as a cricketer. Bradman is the only Australian cricketer to have gotten such an honor. In 1979, the Australian government honored him with the title of a Companion of the Order of Australia. He was called the 'Greatest Cricketer of the Twentieth Century' by the *Wisden Cricket Almanack* in 2000.

Bradman married Jessie Martha Menzies in 1932, after a twelve-year-long courtship. Lady Bradman passed away in 1997 due to cancer. She was 88 years old. Sir Donald Bradman died at the age of 92 on February 25, 2001.

The cricketer wrote a few books in his lifetime. His first book called *Don Bradman's Book—The Story of My Cricketing Life with Hints on Batting, Bowling and Fielding* was published in 1930.

Other books by Bradman include *My Cricketing Life, Farewell to Cricket* and *The Art of Cricket.*

The Royal Australian Mint issued a commemorative gold coin with the image of the cricketer on August 27, 2008. In the following year, Bradman was inducted into the ICC Cricket Hall of Fame.

EDDY MERCKX

BIRTH: June 17, 1945
Meensel-Kiezegem, Belgium

Eddy Merckx is a formerly-professional Belgian, bicycle racer. He competed in 1585 races in his 13-year-long career. He is one of the most celebrated cyclists of all time, with eleven Grand Tour wins, three World Championships and the World Hour Record to his name.

Eddy Merckx's full name is Edouard Louis Joseph Merckx. He was born on June 17, 1945, in Belgium, to Jennie Merckx and Jules Merckx. Eddy began cycling at the mere age of four and got his first racing licence in 1961. He dropped out of school to pursue his passion.

In 1962 he pursuaded his parents to let him

drop out of school to pursue competitive cycling full-time.

It soon proved to be the right choice. In 1962, he entered 55 races as an amateur and won 23 of them, including Belgium's national championship. He soon began to dominate cyclists in other European countries. In 1964 he won the Amateur World Championship Road Race, and the next year he turned professional. His first major victory came in 1966, before he was even 21, at the Milan-San Remo cycle race in Italy.

Merckx won Belgium's national championship and was beginning to dominate the sport. His next victory came in 1964 at the Amateur World Championship Road Race. The following year he started competing professionally and signed with Rik Van Looy's Belgian team, Solo Superia. During his time with Solo Superia, he took part in more than seventy races.

In 1966, Merckx moved to Peugeot's cycling team and got his first major win as a professional at the Milan San Remo cycle race at the age of twenty. He won twenty races in 1967.

In 1967, Merckx started his first Grand Tour and won several stages of the race. At the end of the year, he was ranked ninth overall. He became the world champion after winning the UCI Road World Championships in the Netherlands, and also won the same in 1971 and 1974. In 1968, he took part in the Giro di Sardegna, which he won. During that season he sadly had to pull out from races like the Paris-Nice race and Tour of Flanders due to a knee injury. Despite that, Merckx attended the 1968 Giro d'Italia race and won. He scored a total of 32 victories that season.

Between 1968–1974, he won the Paris-Nice race, the Tour de France, the G'iro de Italia, and the Vuelta a Levante. He participated in the Paris-Luxemburg cycle race but suffered from an accident that could have been fatal. The riders were to be followed by pacers. Merckx's pacer was Fernand Wambst. A collision occurred between Merckx, his pacer and another pacer. Wambst died in the accident and Merckx was heavily injured; it took him months to recover.

Between 1969 and 1975 Merckx won about half the races he participated in. He was a cycling legend when it came to fitness. An experiment was also conducted on Merckx to study how he managed to race for such long periods. The result showed that he had the ability to maintain his speed even with high levels of lactic acid in his body.

In 1972, Merckx set the record for the greatest distance covered by a cyclist in one hour—49.431 kilometers, or about 30.715 miles. He broke the record in the difficult and high-altitude terrain of the Mexico track. In 1977, Merckx got a new sponsor: FIAT. He started the season by winning the Tour Méditerranéen and Grand Prix d'Aix. He completed the year by winning the Kermis race. Merckx began competing in only a few selected races in order to focus more on his health.

In May 1978, he announced his retirement from bicycle racing. After retirement, he started Eddy Merckx Cycles in 1980. Despite facing many problems, the company went on to achieve success among professional cyclists.

For a decade, Merckx helped manage the World Championships for the Belgian team. Even after he retired, Merckx was involved with the sport in some way or the other. In 2002, Merckx helped in arranging the Tour of Qatar and organized the Tour of Oman road races.

In his entire career, Merckx won over 445 races, which is a record in itself. He is recognized as the first athlete to have covered a record distance with 49.431 km in one hour.

Eddy married Claudine Acou on December 5, 1967. The couple are proud parents of two children. Eddy's son, Axel Merckx, is also a professional cyclist.

KITZBÜHEL

INGEMAR STENMARK

BIRTH: March 18, 1956
Lapland, Sweden

Ingemar Stenmark is a former Swedish alpine ski racer. He set the record with 86 World Cup wins during the fifteen years of his professional career. He is considered as one of the most famous Swedish athletes ever.

Ingemar Stenmark was born on March 18, 1956, in Sweden. He grew up in Tarnaby, which was just a few miles from the Arctic Circle. He used to live with his grandparents on a farm outside Tarnaby before he moved into town. Stenmark got interested in skiing because of his father, Erik Stenmark, who was also a national skier. He started skiing at the age of five and his first coach was his father.

Stenmark was shy and reserved as a kid. He started skiing because it was something he could enjoy alone. He used to ski every day for hours, after school and even during the cold weather. His hard work soon began to pay off. Stenmark was seven when he won his first race. By the age of eight, he'd won his first national competition. In 1965, he was selected for an annual international race in Italy. He placed fourteenth in the race during his first attempt at the slalom race. To focus more on the sport, Stenmark fully committed his time to skiing. He dropped out of school after completing his primary education.

Stenmark started to train with the Swiss junior national team at the age of thirteen. He trained for the worst: the giant slalom on the steeper and the more challenging courses in Italy. In the 1972–73 season, his best ranks were fourth and fifth in the Swedish junior nationals. The next season, Stenmark made significant improvement once he realized he could get more consistent wins by not taking unnecessary risks during the races.

The most significant moment of Stenmark's career came in 1974. He was a part of the European racing circuit and participated in his first ever World Cup event where he placed second in the slalom. Soon after, in December 1974, he got his first World Cup victory with the slalom at Madonna di Campiglio in Italy. In the 1978–79 season he won a total of thirteen slalom races, a record no one has managed to beat.

After he won three back-to-back world cup titles, he was viewed as a star in Sweden. He also received the highest Swedish honor, a special gold medal, bestowed upon him by Sweden's King Carl XVI Gustaf. However, for Stenmark, the year 1979 did not end well. He suffered from a concussion and sustained injuries during a training run on the Italian Alps in September 1979. It took him three weeks to recover in the hospital. Soon after, during the 1979–80 World Cup, Stenmark won ten races. He again took both the slalom and giant slalom titles, but he lost the World Cup by six points and came in second instead. In 1980, he participated in the Winter Olympics held at Lake Placid, New York. He won gold medals for both slalom and giant slalom.

In 1981, he won the gold medal in the slalom and got silver in the giant slalom at the World Championship in Schladming. In the 1982 World Championship in Austria, he got the silver medal in the giant slalom, and a gold medal in the slalom, finishing second overall.

The year 1984 was an unfortunate one for Stenmark. He was not allowed to participate in the 1984 Olympic games due to the technicalities of his sponsorship contract. In 1988, he was again allowed to compete in the Olympics once he had taken care of his endorsement contracts. However, Stenmark was not in his best form that season. In 1989, he announced his retirement from the sport.

Stenmark has been married thrice. His first marriage was to Ann Ufhagen, which lasted until

1988. His last marriage was in 2016; he married his long-time girlfriend, Tarja Olli. He is the father of two daughters.

With his notable achievements in sports, Stenmark became a national icon for sports in Sweden from 1976 to 1978.

JESSE OWENS

BIRTH: September 12, 1913
Oakville, Alabama, USA

DEATH: March 31, 1980 (aged 66)
Phoenix, Arizona, USA

Jesse Owens was an American track-and-field athlete known for his world record in the 1936 Berlin Olympic Games, in which he won four gold medals. He also made a world record in the long jump which remained unbroken for 25 years.

Jesse Owens' full name was James Cleveland Owens. He was born to Henry Cleveland Owens and Emma Fitzgerald on September 12, 1913, in Oakville, Alabama.

When he was eight, "JC" (Owens' nickname) moved to Cleveland, Ohio with his family. At the age of nine, on his first day at a public school, his teacher misheard "JC" as "Jesse" because of his strong Southern accent. That's how the name Jesse Owens stuck with him for the rest of his life.

By the age of seven, Owens started to work in his spare time. He went to Fairmount Junior High School for his early education. There he met Charles Riley, his high school track coach. His coach allowed Jesse to practice before school, making allowances for his work schedule.

Jesse started his career as a track-and-field athlete in 1928. Throughout high school, he won every event he participated in, including the Ohio state championship three years in a row. The competition which gained Jesse immense attention was the 1933 National High School Championship in Chicago. He had set a new high school world record by running the 100 yards dash in 9.4 seconds.

Even though he was a student, Owens had already set the world record in the 100 and

220-yard runs and did remarkably well in long jumps. After he graduated high school, he was scouted by many colleges, but Jesse chose Ohio State University.

In 1935, he took part in the Big Ten Championships and broke three world records and won four individual events. Just before the competition, Owens suffered from a sore back, and his coach wanted him to rest instead of participating. He didn't practice for many weeks before the competition but still made history. This boosted Owens' confidence to take part in bigger competitions.

Owens entered the 1936 Berlin Summer Olympics marking his most legendary accomplishments. Adolf Hitler had meant to use the Olympics as a device to justify the dominance of the German Aryans as a higher race. But Owens challenged his opinion when he became the first American track-and-field athlete to win four gold medals in one Olympic games. He became a role model for many people in that era, when race was a highly debated issue. The long jump record he set in the 1936 Olympics lasted for 25 years.

In Berlin, Owens received sponsorship from the Adidas shoe company. He became quite popular and was also asked to compete in Sweden. But Owens returned to his own country. He thought he would receive some profitable commercial deals after his Olympics win, but due to prevailing racial tensions, he got a very different reaction in his home country. He didn't receive any awards from President Roosevelt, who also did not congratulate Owens on his success, as was customary. Owens left university and focused on finding a job to earn money. He was forced to take part in various events (like racing against horses and cars) and played with the Harlem Globetrotters to make a living.

After retirement from amateur athletics, Owens dabbled in boys' guidance activities and was offered a chance to become a US goodwill ambassador. He also served as a secretary for the Illinois State Athletic Commission.

Owens was a loving husband to his wife Ruth Solomon, whom he married in 1932 and was married to for nearly 48 years. The couple was blessed with three daughters. He died on March 31, 1980, due to lung cancer.

Jesse was honored later in life in the manner in which he deserved. In 1970, he got inducted to the Alabama Sports Hall of Fame. In 1976, he was finally awarded the Presidential Medal of Freedom. Many honors were bestowed upon him after his death. In 1990, he was presented with the highest expression of national appreciation, the Congressional Gold Medal. An asteroid discovered the same year was named after him. Owens was depicted on two US postage stamps. Many streets, schools, parks and stadiums are named after him as a tribute.

LEBRON JAMES

BIRTH: December 30, 1984
Akron, Ohio, USA

LeBron Raymone James is an American basketball player, considered to be one of the greatest basketball players of all time.

LeBron was born on December 30, 1984, in Akron, Ohio, to Gloria James and Anthony McClelland. LeBron's childhood was tough, as he grew up in a poor neighborhood. He had always had an interest in sports, especially basketball. His idol was Michael Jordan, whom he watched in his early days to learn the game.

Considering their unstable lifestyle, Gloria decided to let the young LeBron move in with

Frankie Walker's family. Walker introduced James to basketball at the age of nine. While he stayed with the Walker family, LeBron became more disciplined and started to attend school regularly. After he completed his elementary school studies, he started attending St Vincent–St Mary High School, a private school, in 1999. The school noticed his talent and asked LeBron to join the school team. LeBron led his team to win three state titles.

LeBron scored more than two thousand points in just four years. He even appeared on the cover of *Sports Illustrated* and the *ESPN* magazine. He decided not to attend college after high school and went straight to the National Basketball Association (NBA) league.

LeBron started his professional basketball career in 2003. He was the first pick made by the Cleveland Cavaliers in the NBA draft. He ended up playing his first seven seasons with them. He was a strong forward in the game. His average in the game was twenty points. The same year, he became the youngest person to win the 'Rookie of the Year' title. At nineteen, LeBron was the youngest member of the team in the 2004 Athens Olympics, although he hardly played that season. He continued to shine in 2005 and became the youngest player to score more than fifty points in one game.

In 2006, he continued to help his team reach new heights. His team, the Cleveland Cavaliers played against the Washington Wizards. They defeated the Wizards in the first round, but the team didn't go on to win the finals. The same year, LeBron renewed his contract with the Cavaliers for $60 million.

Even though the team's rank was not that good, LeBron was named the 'All-Star Game MVP' in the 2007–08 season. He was the only player with an average of thirty points per game. It was the highest in NBA's regular season.

In 2008, LeBron was selected for the US Olympic basketball team, for which he went to Beijing. The team won the finals against Spain and brought home the gold medal. In 2010, LeBron became a free agent, with most teams wanting him to join them.

LeBron decided to join the Miami Heat for his next season. He finished second that season and scored an average of 26.7 points per game. The 2011–12 season was a major success for the team with their win over the Oklahoma City Thunder in the NBA finals, earning LeBron his first title. In 2012, he participated in his third Olympic games, in London, and brought home gold for the second time.

At the age of 28, LeBron became the youngest player to score 20,000 points and beat Kobe Bryant's previous record. He also led his team to their second consecutive national championship title. In 2014, LeBron returned to the Cavaliers and ended his contract with the Miami Heat.

However, the 2014–15 season was not a good one for LeBron. He suffered from back and knee problems due to which he missed 13 out of 82 regular season games. But, LeBron still led the Cavaliers to the NBA finals that season. He became the first player in nearly fifty years to have reached the final round in five back-to-back seasons. In the following years, LeBron's injuries only got worse. However, this didn't stop him from breaking records. At the age of 33, LeBron became the youngest player to reach 30,000 points.

Apart from his phenomenal athletic career, LeBron James is involved in many charitable projects. He founded the LeBron James Family Foundation in 2004. The foundation helps single-parent families and unprivileged children. He also supports the Boys & Girls Club of America, Children's Defense Fund, and ONEXONE.

LeBron married his high school sweetheart Savannah Brinson in 2013, in San Diego. The couple has three children, two sons and one daughter.

LIONEL MESSI

BIRTH: June 24, 1987
Rosario, Argentina

Lionel Messi is an Argentinean football player who has been named the FIFA 'World Player of the Year' five times. He is also the first player to win three European Golden Shoes.

Lionel Messi was born Luis Lionel Andres Messi on June 24, 1987, in Rosario, Argentina to Jorge Messi and Celia Cuccittini. At the mere age of five, Messi started to play for Grandoli, a local football club coached by his father. By the time he turned eight, he was playing for the youth academy of Newell's Old Boys, a major professional football squad in Rosario.

Messi was smaller than most of the kids in his age group. At the age of eleven, he was diagnosed with a growth hormone deficiency. The treatment was costly, so his father went to several Argentinean football clubs for financial aid. The coach of FC Barcelona, Carles Rexach came to his aid and offered Messi a contract and promised to pay for his medical bills—only if they moved to Spain. Messi signed the contract and joined FC Barcelona's youth academy.

Messi officially started his football career in 2000 in the under-14 team. He scored 21 goals in 14 games for the junior team.

At the age of sixteen, Messi made his informal debut for FC Barcelona in a friendly match. At just seventeen years of age, he became the youngest player to play and score in the Spanish La Liga 2004–05 season. The same year Messi acquired Spanish citizenship, which made it possible for him to make a debut in the UEFA Champions League. He managed to strike six goals in the season in a total of seventeen games. But Messi had to leave the championship midway due to a muscle tear in his thigh. Barcelona went on to win the league that season.

From 2007, Messi was no longer a backup player in the matches. He was one of official eleven members in the team. In the 26 league games, he successfully netted the ball fourteen times. He even scored a hat-trick in El Clasico, becoming the youngest ever to pull this off. He was dubbed "Messidona" because his way of scoring was very similar to Maradona's, who is considered to be one of the greatest footballers of all times.

In 2007, he sustained a muscle tear injury for the fourth time in three seasons. The club hired a personal physiotherapist for Messi so he would recover faster.

The years 2008 and 2009 spelled success for Messi. He helped his team win the La Liga in 2008 and 2009 and eventually the Champions League in 2009. FC Barcelona achieved their first ever 'treble' (a team winning three trophies in a single season or calendar year). Messi ended the season with 38 goals overall in 51 matches, besting Ronaldo for the FIFA 'World Player of the Year' honor. He also won the European Golden Shoe award for being Europe's top scorer.

In 2010, Messi continued to grow as a professional football player. In the 2011–12 season Messi broke records upon records. At the age of 24, he became the club's best scorer of all time, surpassing Cesar Rodriguez's record of 232 goals. He also exceeded Gerd Muller's 85 goals in club and international play by scoring 91 goals by the end of 2012. In January 2013, he made history after getting named the FIFA Ballon d'Or winner for the fourth time. He also led Barcelona to the 2011 Champions League title.

Messi declared his retirement from international football following Argentina's second consecutive loss to Chile in the Copa America final of 2016. However, fans started a campaign to convince him to change his decision and they succeeded. Messi agreed to be a part of the Argentinean team for the 2018 World Cup.

Messi's considerate nature extends to a lot of charitable work as well. In 2007, he formed the

Leo Messi Foundation, a charity which supports children through health care, education, and sports. Because he faced many medical ailments in his childhood, he wanted to help children who were going through the same trials. His charity covers the transport, hospital and other costs for sick children. In 2010, he worked with UNICEF as their goodwill ambassador to support children's rights. In 2013, Messi donated a large sum of money for the renovation of the Victor Vilela Children's Hospital in his Rosario, in Argentina.

Messi married his long-time girlfriend Antonella Roccuzzo in June 2017. They knew each other since Leo was only five years old but only began dating in 2008. The couple has two sons, Thiago and Mateo.

MAGNUS CARLSEN

BIRTH: November 30, 1990
Tønsberg, Norway

Magnus Carlsen is a Norwegian chess player who currently holds the world chess champion title. At the age of 22, Magnus was the second youngest world chess champion.

Sven Magnus Øen Carlsen was born on November 30, 1990 in Norway to Sigrun Øen and Henrik Albert Carlsen. Magnus displayed advanced mental capabilities from a very young age. At the age of four, he could assemble Lego sets intended for much older children. His father recognized his son's abilities and was the first person to introduce him to the game. Magnus' father taught him chess even though he himself was an amateur chess player.

In 1999, at the age of eight, Magnus participated in his first chess competition at the Norwegian Chess Championship in the junior category. He played eleven games and maintained a score of 6.5 points. Given his talent, the International Grandmaster Peter Heine Nielsen started coaching Magnus.

During the year 2000, Carlsen honed his skills even further, gaining over a thousand rating points and a performance rating of around 2000. By the end of 2002, he'd competed in more than 300 chess tournaments.

In 2004, Carlsen gained international recognition after he won his first tournament in the C group in the Corus chess tournament, at Wijk aan Zee in Netherlands. He played in the lowest-rated group against adult players, but he dominated the tournament. This victory by the teenager led Grandmaster Lubomir Kavalek to dub him the "Mozart of Chess".

Carlsen had played against champions like Anatoly Karpov—beating the former world champion—and Garry Kasparov, who was one of the top-ranked chess players then. Carlsen ranked second at the 2004 Dubai Open Chess Championship in April 2004, leading him to earn the title of Grandmaster. He was the third youngest person ever to have this honor, at the age of thirteen.

At the age of fifteen, Carlsen proved his brilliance by defeating the number ten, Alexei Shirov in 2005. He participated in the 2006 Norwegian Chess Championship, playing fiercely but losing to Berge Østenstad in the final round. In 2007, Carlsen was part of the great Linares chess tournament for the first time. This tournament is known as "the Wimbledon of chess" by many. He finished in second place after playing against stars like Veselin Topalov, Viswanathan Anand, Peter Svidler and Levon Aronian. He was also successful at the Biel International Chess

Festival's Grandmaster Tournament.

Carlsen became the youngest person to ever have won a category 18 tournament in August 2007. At the 37th Chess Olympiad, his rating passed the 2700 mark. In 2008, he finally entered the top ten rankings in the world. Carlsen shared the first place in the Corus chess tournament, which made him the youngest person ever to have won a category 20 tournament.

In 2009, Carlsen's biggest success came after he won the World Blitz Championship and became the fifth (and youngest) chess player to achieve an Elo-rating of over 2800. He then participated in the London Chess Classic and defeated the world champion, Vladimir Kramnik. As a result of his constant success, the nineteen-year-old Carlsen was announced as the top player in the world by FIDE in January 2010; once again the youngest player to achieve this feat.

The world witnessed one of the most important chess matches in the year 2013. It was between Carlsen and the then world chess champion,

Vishwanathan Anand. Carlsen defeated Anand in ten games and thus became the new world champion. At the age of 22, he was the second youngest player to have won the world title, after Gary Kasparov.

For Magnus, the year 2017 had a rough start. He took part in the 79th Tata Steel Chess Tournament but lost the match. His opponent Giri described it as the "most embarrassing moment" of Carlsen's career. Subsequently his ranking also dropped. However, he came back in form after a few months of training. He won the World Blitz Chess Championship for the third time, placed second in the Sinquefield Cup, and fifth in the London Chess Classics, gaining enough points to join the 2017 Grand Chess Tour.

Carlsen's exceptional skills and success have won him five Chess Oscars in his career. In 2011, he received the Peer Gynt Prize, a Norwegian honor for a person or institution that has achieved distinction in society. Carlsen is known for his Elo rating—2882, the highest in chess history.

MARIA SHARAPOVA

BIRTH: April 19, 1987
Nyagan, Russia

Maria Sharapova is a world-famous professional tennis player from Russia. She was the first Russian woman to win the Wimbledon and has held the world number one ranking many times.

Maria Yuryevna Sharapova was born on April 19, 1987 in Nyagan, Russia to Yuri and Yelena Sharapova. In 1989, at the age of two, Sharapova's interest in tennis bloomed when her parents handed her an old racket and started teaching her how to hit the ball.

In 1994, young Sharapova moved to the US with her father and attempted to join the prestigious Nick Bollettieri Tennis Academy. However, she was rejected as the enrollment was based on invitation, and seven-year-old Sharapova was too young anyway. They decided to remain in Florida and a coach was hired for Sharapova. At the age of nine, Sharapova went back to the Bollettieri Academy and did so well on her try-out that she received a full scholarship. The Academy was a part of a talent agency, the International Management Group.

Maria won the Eddie Herr International Junior Tennis Championship at the age of thirteen and was awarded the 'Rising Star' award. In 2001, at the age of fourteen, she turned professional. In 2002 she competed at the Junior Wimbledon and Australian Open tournaments and reached the finals. Because of her young age, she was only allowed to play selected matches and mostly participated in the junior competitions.

In 2003, Sharapova won the WTA title at the Japan Open Tennis Championship and received the WTA 'Newcomer of the Year' award. She played her first Grand Slam, participating in every event. By the end of the year, Sharapova was in the Top 50 list.

In 2004, at the age of seventeen, Sharapova defeated defending champion Serena Williams in the Wimbledon finals to win her first Grand Slam. She became Russia's second female Wimbledon champion to have won the singles title. She entered the Top 10 ranking for the first time in her career. In 2005, Sharapova competed in the Australian Open, Wimbledon and the US Open, reaching the semi-finals in all three events. She became the first Russian woman to hold the world No. 1 ranking the same year.

In 2006, she won her second Grand Slam in the US Open, and the phrase "Maria Mania" was dubbed as a consequence of her achievements. In 2008, she claimed her third Grand Slam title at the Australian Open.

Unfortunately, Sharapova couldn't maintain her No. 1 position due to an injury diagnosed later that year—a torn rotator cuff. She underwent corrective surgery and couldn't play in the later part of the year. After the surgery, she kept away from the sport to focus solely on her recovery.

Sharapova returned to the court in mid-2009, but until 2011 there were no major wins for the player. She did win several WTA titles but lost out on the Grand Slam. Sharapova made her comeback in 2012 and won her first French Open title. She participated in the 2012 London Olympics and won the silver medal. In 2013, her shoulder injury resurfaced and significantly affected her performance. She was forced to miss the last six months of the season.

In 2014, Sharapova won her second French Open and fifth overall Grand Slam title. In 2015, she reached the Australian Open finals and the semi-finals of the US Open, and was ranked fourth at the end of the year.

In March 2016, Sharapova revealed that she had been taking a heart medication—mildronate, which was another name for meldonium, a drug that had recently been banned by the World

Anti-doping Agency. She said that she didn't know about the relation between the two drugs, and had hence failed a drug test. Despite the explanation, the International Tennis Federation (ITF) suspended Sharapova for two years. After an appeal, her sentence was reduced to fifteen months. Sharapova returned to the game in April 2017 and announced her retirement in February 2020, at the age of 32.

Apart from tennis, Sharapova has dedicated her time to charitable projects, and worked with UNDP from 2007. She founded the Maria Sharapova Foundation to help children around the world achieve their dreams. She established a range of lifestyle products called Sugarpova in 2012. A percentage of the sales from her business goes to her foundation. In 2017, Sharapova released her autobiography titled *Unstoppable: My Life So Far.*

MARY KOM

BIRTH: March 1, 1983
Manipur, India

Mary Kom is a five-time World Boxing Champion and the only boxer to have won a medal in each one of the seven world championships. She is famously known as "Magnificent Mary" and "MC Mary Kom".

Mary Kom was born on March 1, 1983 in Manipur, India, to Mangte Tonpa Kom and Mangte Akham Kom. They were a family of poor farmers. Due to her family's financial condition, Mary had to work hard from a very young age. She used to work on the farms and also attend Loktak Christian Model High School. As the eldest of four siblings, she also had to take care of her younger siblings.

Mary later moved to St. Xavier Catholic School. But Mary only studied there until the eighth grade, always more interested in sports than academics. She participated in all types of sports in school except for boxing, ironically. Mary took up boxing after getting inspired by the famous Manipuri boxer, Dingko Singh. He was a great athlete who won gold at the Asian Games in 1998. When Mary started boxing, she kept it a secret from her family. The reason being that boxing was not considered an appropriate sport for women and would potentially reduce her chances of finding a good groom.

To receive proper training, Kom decided to move to Imphal, in 1998, at the age of fifteen. She joined the Sports Academy in Imphal and there she met the state coach, Narjit Singh.

Kom officially started her boxing career in 2000. She won the Women's Boxing Championship in Manipur and a regional competition in West Bengal. After winning many matches in her motherland, she started to participate at the international level. At the age of eighteen, Kom obtained a silver medal in her first AIBA Women's World Boxing Championship in the United States. In 2002, she won a gold medal at the second AIBA Women's World Boxing Championship in Turkey. In 2003, Kom won gold at the 2003 Asian Boxing Championship in Hissar. The India government honored her with the Arjuna Award the same year. Kom showed her passion and talent for boxing when she secured a total of five consecutive National Championships from 2000 to 2005. She won the AIBA world boxing championship, in 2002 and 2006.

Kom took a year-long break from boxing to fulfill her family responsibilities. After she gained her family's support, she returned to boxing again in 2008. Kom trained day and night to rebuild her stamina and strength. She made a comeback in full form in the 2008 Asian Women's Boxing Championship, winning silver. She won her fourth gold at the AIBA Women's World Boxing Championship in China. In 2009, she won gold again at the Asian Indoor Games in Vietnam.

In 2010, she earned her fifth consecutive gold in the AIBA Women's Boxing competition and one in the Asian Women's Boxing Championships in Kazakhstan.

The year 2012 was historic, for both Kom and her home country India. Kom became the first Indian woman to represent India in boxing at the Olympics. She won the bronze medal and became the third Indian woman to win an individual medal at the Olympics. Another major feat by Kom was winning the gold medal in the 2014 Incheon Asian Games. For her significant contribution to sports, she was awarded the Padma Shri in 2006. And in 2013 she received the third highest civilian award of India, the Padma Bhushan.

Kom has opened many doors for women in India and encouraged them to achieve their dreams. She started an academy in Manipur that teaches self-defense to young children. Mary co-authored her autobiography, *Unbreakable*, documenting her life struggles and how she rose to success. The book was published by Harper

Collins in 2013. In 2014, a biopic of Kom's life, *Mary Kom,* was released starring Priyanka Chopra. Kom strongly supports animal rights and does voluntary work for PETA India.

Mary married K Onler Kom in 2005 after dating him for four years. Onler first met Mary in New Delhi when she was on her way to the National Games. They are now the proud parents of three sons.

MICHAEL JORDAN

BIRTH: February 17, 1963
New York City, USA

Michael Jordan, also known as "Air Jordan", is a former American basketball player. He is the greatest all-round player in the history of the sport. He is best known for his wildly famous dunk shot.

Michael Jeffrey Jordan was born on February 17, 1963, in Brooklyn, New York, to James and Deloris Jordan. From a very young age, he shared a special bond with his father; baseball was their first love. However, Jordan pursued basketball after getting inspired by his older brother Larry, his idol and a fantastic athlete.

Jordan attended Laney High School in North Carolina where he played for the school's junior team. Jordan performed exceptionally well in every game, and eventually, his coaches noticed his talent. He was selected for the McDonald's All-American Team, the best of all high school basketball teams.

In 1981, Jordan was offered a scholarship by the University of North Carolina. He started training under the famous coach, Dean Smith. UNC won the NCAA Division I championship in 1982, with Jordan scoring the final basket against Georgetown. He was named the "College Player of the Year" by Sporting News in 1983.

In 1984, Jordan participated in his first Olympic Games as a part of the US Olympic basketball team, and soon after got drafted by the Chicago Bulls. He took the team to the playoffs and averaging about 33 points per game, Jordan was named the NBA 'Rookie of the Year' and was chosen for the All-Star game. He scored a place in the All-NBA Second Team. In 1985, Jordan successfully graduated with a degree in geography. Sadly, he suffered a foot injury in his second season. The Chicago Bulls won the game, but Jordan was out for 64 games that season.

The 1986–87 season saw Jordan breaking major records. Jordan scored 40 or more points in nine consecutive games and 23 straight in one game, creating an NBA record. He was recognized as the Slam Dunk Champion. Jordan scored 3000 points in a single season, becoming the first player to do so since Wilt Chamberlain. He continued playing for the next seven years but surprisingly announced his "retirement" in 1993 stating that he had lost the will to play the game.

During this break, Jordan pursued his dream of playing baseball. Sadly, he was not successful as a baseball player. In 1995, Jordan returned to the basketball scene. He made his comeback with the world's shortest press release, consisting of only two words, "I'm back." His comeback game was one of the highest-rated televised games. In the 1995–96 season, the Bulls finished with a score of 72–10 earning Jordan his eighth scoring title. He won the MVP award again that year, and Jordan's career continued to rise over the next few years.

Jordan retired again after the 1997-98 season. He became the president of basketball operations for the Washington Wizards in 2000. He ended up playing for the team for two years before retiring for good in 2003. In 2003, Jordan became the first person above the age of forty to score forty points in an NBA game.

Jordan collaborated with Nike to create his signature sneakers. Soon, the demand for his Air Jordans was unbelievably high. He also signed deals with other major companies like Gatorade, McDonald's, Wheaties, and MCI.

The talented athlete received several NBA titles from 1984–88 including "Defensive Player of the

Year" and "Slam Dunk Contest Champion". In 1996, NBA named him as one of the fifty greatest players of all time. He has also been inducted to the Naismith Memorial Basketball Hall of Fame in 2009. In 2016, Jordan was awarded the Presidential Medal of Freedom by President Barack Obama.

Jordan was involved with charitable work alongside his basketball career. From 2001 to 2014, Jordan held an annual charity golfing event known as the Michael Jordan Celebrity Invitational. The gathered donations were used to help out foundations like Make-a-wish, Cats Care and Opportunity Village.

In 1989, Jordan got married to Juanita Vanoy. But after seventeen years of marriage, the couple separated. He got married for the second time in 2013 to model Yvette Prieto. Jordan is the father of five children.

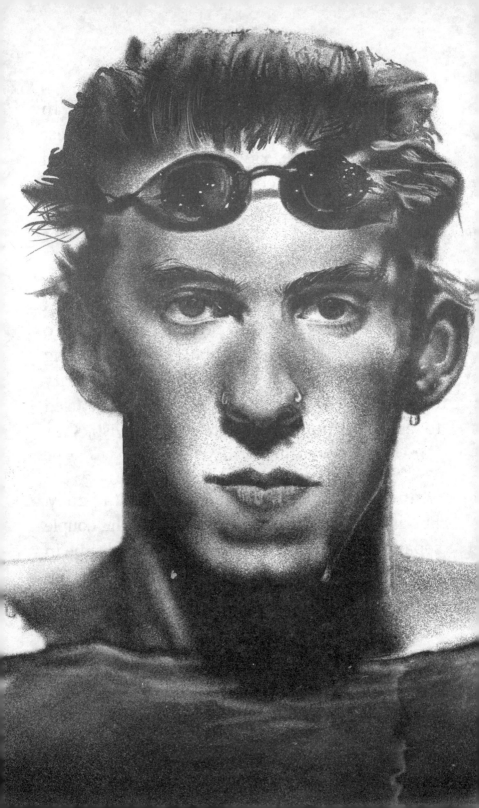

MICHAEL PHELPS

BIRTH: June 30, 1985
Baltimore, Maryland, USA

Michael Phelps is a retired American swimmer who set the record for the most Olympic medals won by any athlete in history.

Michael Fred Phelps II was born in Baltimore, Maryland, on June 30, 1985, to Fred and Debbie Phelps. Following in his elder sisters' footsteps, Phelps began to swim at the age of seven. Initially, Phelps was scared of putting his face in the water, so his instructors allowed him to float around the pool on his back. This way, he soon mastered the backstroke in swimming. When he was eleven, he started training under Bob Bowman, who he met at the North Baltimore Aquatic Club. After he realized Phelps' potential, Coach Bowman designed an intensive training program for him. Soon, Phelps was selected for the US National B Team in 1999.

Phelps' swimming career started at the age of fifteen in the year 2000. He was selected for the US Summer Olympics swimming team. Phelps became the youngest male swimmer in 68 years to represent America at the Olympics. He finished at the fifth position in the 200-meter butterfly swimming category.

In 2001, Phelps set the world record for the 200-meter butterfly, becoming the youngest male swimmer to set a swimming world record when he posted 1 min 54.92 sec in the 200-metre butterfly. Later that year, during the 2001 World Aquatic Championships in Fukuoka, he broke his own record and won his first international medal. In 2002, Phelps participated in the Pan-Pacific Swimming Championships and won three gold medals and two silver medals.

In 2003, Phelps took part in the World Championships and the US spring nationals. He made history when he won the 200-meter freestyle, 200-meter backstroke, and the 100-meter butterfly in the US Nationals. Phelps was the first American male swimmer to have won three different races with three different strokes at a national championship.

In the 2004 Olympics in Athens, Phelps won six gold medals and two bronze medals, tying with Aleksandr Dityatin for the record of the most medals won in a single Olympics. He even broke his own world record in the 400-meter race.

In the November after the Athens games, Phelps was arrested for drunk-driving, and served an eighteen months' probation period, paid a fine and had to do community service. He started attending the University of Michigan, following coach Bowman there, to study sports marketing and management.

Phelps was soon off his probation and continued to dominate the swimming world. He got a total of six medals, five gold and one silver, at the 2005 World Championships. At the 2007 World Championship, he participated in eight events and won seven gold medals. He made world record time in five of them.

Phelps created history during the 2008 Olympics in Beijing. He won eight gold medals in a single Olympics, breaking Mark Spitz's record made in 1972. Every gold medal he won set a new world record, apart from the 100-meter butterfly which set an Olympic record.

During the 2009 World Championships, Phelps lost a race for the first time in four years to a relative newcomer. In the 2011 World Championships Phelps lost two gold medals to underdog Ryan Lochte. However, he did win four gold medals, which bolstered his confidence, and he started working determinedly towards the 2012 London Olympics. He had made it clear early on that he did not wish to swim past the age of thirty, and would retire after the 2012 Olympics.

In 2012, Phelps won four gold medals and once again, he broke the record for most Olympic medals earned—his total was 22. After a short retirement he made a proper comeback in the 2016 Rio de Janeiro Olympics as the American flag-bearer in the opening ceremony. He earned his 23rd gold medal in the first event in Rio. Phelps announced his retirement once again, two days after his fifth Olympics.

Phelps founded the Michael Phelps Foundation in 2008 to nurture interest in swimming as a sport amongst the youth and promote a healthy lifestyle. Phelps is also a great writer. He released two books called *Beneath the Surface: My Story* and *No Limits: The Will to Succeed.*

Phelps married former Miss California, Nicole Johnson in 2016. The couple has two children.

MICHAEL SCHUMACHER

BIRTH: January 3, 1969
Hürth-Hermülhein, Germany

Michael Schumacher is a famous retired German Formula One racer. Schumacher holds the record for the most Formula One (F1) Grand Prix race victories and F1 series championships.

Michael Schumacher was born on January 3, 1969, near Cologne, Germany to Rolf and Elisabeth Schumacher. Michael started to take an interest in racing at a very young age. When he was four, Michael's father gave him a kart powered by an old lawn-mower engine. His interest in go-karting piqued, encouraged by his father who was a part of the management team of a go-kart track. Michael soon won his first kart championship.

Michael started his career at the age of twelve. He won his first German Junior Karting Championship in 1984. By the end of 1987, Michael had gained both European and German karting competition titles.

In 1988, the teen racer left karting and started driving Formula Three (F3) cars instead. His car racing career started when he won the Formula Koenig. In 1990, Michael graduated to the German Formula 3 league. He was placed in the Mercedes junior racing program and competed in the World Sports Prototype Championship as a part of this group. Under the guidance of Jochen Neerspasch and Jochen Mass, Michael learned much of what would later be known as his trademark smooth style.

Schumacher started his Formula One career in 1991. He made his debut at the Belgium Grand Prix with the Jordan team, finishing the race in the seventh position. After one race and a legal battle, Schumacher left Jordan for the Benetton team. With Benetton, Schumacher won his first race in Belgium and finished third overall in his very first year in F1. In 1993, he won the Portuguese Grand Prix and finished fourth overall in the championship.

In 1994, at the age of 25, Schumacher won the FIA Formula One Driver's World Championship by only one point. After a controversial collision with Damon Hill in the final race, Schumacher was accused of cheating.

In 1995, he won the Formula One championship. He won 8 races in 1994, and 9 races in 1995. In 1996, Michael decided to join the Italian Ferrari team, which had not produced a champion in two decades. In his first season with Ferrari, Schumacher participated in the 1996 World Championship and finished third.

In 2000, Schumacher became Ferrari's first champion in 21 years. Schumacher dominated the Formula 1 scene by winning the title five years in a row. In 2001 he won nine races, and in 2002 he won eleven races. He broke Juan Fangio's record for the most F1 titles held with a grand total of seven F1 titles to his name.

The year 2005 came with a major change in the world of racing. It was declared that the drivers had to use the same set of tires for the entire race. Ferrari used Bridgestone tires, which needed to be replaced often, but were safer. As a result, the teams that used Michelin tires won most of the races, since they didn't require frequent replacements. Schumacher only won one competition that season, the United States Grand Prix, coming in third overall. He retired for four years after completing his 2006 Formula One season. Following his retirement, he worked with Ferrari as an assistant to the CEO and as an advisor to the team. At that point he had already broken the record for the most races won, bringing his total to 91 (the earlier record being 51, held by Alain Prost).

Schumacher made a comeback in F1 in 2010, only with the Mercedes team this time. His retirement had made him somewhat rusty, and during his three seasons with Mercedes he didn't win a single race, never finishing on a rank higher than eighth in the overall F1 standings.

In 2012 Michael Schumacher announced retirement once again. The first year into his retirement, Schumacher hit his head on a rock while skiing in France and sustained severe head injuries, despite having worn a helmet. He was in a coma for several months following the accident, and is still recovering from memory loss and paralysis.

Schumacher also worked for many charitable causes. He donated 1.5 million euros to UNESCO and funded the construction of 'Palace for the Poor' in Peru, supporting education and medical treatment for homeless children, and development programs to decrease poverty. He was named special ambassador for UNESCO in 2002 and made headlines for his $10 million donation to the relief effort for the Indian Ocean tsunami of 2004.

Schumacher got married to Corinna Betsch in August 1995. The couple have a daughter and a son.

MUHAMMAD ALI

BIRTH: *January 17, 1942*
Louisville, Kentucky, USA

DEATH: *June 3, 2016*
Scottsdale, Arizona, USA

Muhammad Ali was an American professional boxer and a social activist. Ali was the first fighter to win the world heavyweight championship on three separate occasions. He was universally considered to be one of the greatest athletes of the twentieth century and dubbed as "The Greatest".

Muhammad Ali's real name was Cassius Marcellus Clay, Jr. He was born on January 17, 1942, in Louisville, Kentucky, to Cassius Marcellus Clay, Sr. and Odessa Grady Clay. Ali grew up in Kentucky where racism was very prominent. The discrimination that came with it made life difficult for African-Americans like Ali.

Ali discovered his talent for boxing through a weird turn of fate. At the age of twelve, his bike got stolen. He reported the theft to a local police officer, Joe Martin, threatening to beat up the culprit. Martin, who taught boxing at the local youth center, suggested that Ali learn the art first before issuing challenges. Soon, they both realized that Ali possessed natural talent for the sport.

Ali started his boxing career when he was only a teenager. He won his first amateur bout in 1954, and went on to win the 1956 Golden Gloves tournament in the light heavyweight class. In 1959, he won the National Golden Gloves Tournament of Champions and the Amateur Athletic Union's national title for the light heavyweight division.

In 1960 Ali was selected for the US Olympic boxing team in Rome. He won the light heavyweight gold medal and returned home an American hero. He decided to turn professional with the support of the Louisville Sponsoring Group.

In 1964, Ali became the youngest person to achieve the World Heavyweight Champion title. He then joined the black Muslim group, the Nation of Islam, and changed his name to Muhammad Ali. He eventually converted to orthodox Islam in the 1970s. Due to his religious beliefs, he refused to serve in the US army after being drafted in 1967. This led to Ali getting arrested and losing his world title and boxing license immediately. After three and a half years his ban was lifted, and he was allowed to return to the ring. Ali returned to the ring after the hiatus with a win against Jerry Quarry in 1970.

In the early 1970s, he fought some of his most epic fights. The first one was called the Fight of the Century. He fought against Joe Frazier for the heavyweight title but lost in the fifteenth round. It was Ali's first professional defeat after 31 wins. Another major fight was called the Rumble in the Jungle, in 1974, between Ali and George Foreman. Ali won the match and regained the heavyweight title.

In 1978, Ali was defeated by the newcomer Leon Spinks, losing his title. However, seven months later, Ali defeated Spinks in a rematch, regaining his title. Ali retired from boxing in 1981 with a career record of 56 wins, five losses and 37 knockouts.

After his retirement, Ali dedicated most of his time to charitable causes. For his philanthropic work, he was awarded the Presidential Medal of Freedom in 2005 by President George Bush. In 1997, Ali opened the Muhammad Ali Parkinson Center at the Barrow Neurological Institute in Arizona. In 1998, he became a United Nations Messenger of Peace.

For his exceptional work in the field of sports, he was honored with titles like "The Greatest",

"Fighter of the Year", "Sportsman of the Year", "Sportsman of the Century" and "Sports Personality of the Century". He got inducted to the International Boxing Hall of Fame in 1990.

In 1984, Ali was diagnosed with Parkinson's disease. In his autobiography, *The Soul of a Butterfly: Reflections on Life's Journey*, he described his life after retirement. The condition eventually made it difficult for him to even communicate well.

Ali was married four times in his life. He had nine children. Ali's fourth wife, Lonnie (née Yolanda Williams) had known him since they were children. They remained married until Ali's death. Ali died on June 3, 2016, in Arizona, USA at the age of 74. He was one of the most recognizable personalities of the twentieth century. Because of his courage and discipline, he remains one of the best-known sportsmen in the world.

NADIA COMĂNECI

BIRTH: November 12, 1961
Oneşti, Romania

Nadia Comăneci is a Romanian gymnast who created history as the first gymnast to score a perfect ten in an Olympic gymnastics event. She was also the youngest all-around Olympic gold medalist at the mere age of fourteen.

Nadia Elena Comăneci was born on November 12, 1961, in Romania to Gheorghe and Stefania Comăneci. At the age of six, Nadia started training in gymnastics under the duo Bela and Martha Karolyi at their world-renowned experimental gymnastics school.

In 1969, Comăneci participated in her first gymnastics competition, the Romanian National Junior Championship. She placed thirteenth that year. In 1970, Comăneci won the competition and became the youngest gymnast ever to win the Romanian Nationals. The following year, she expanded her talents to international platforms. In 1972, she won three gold medals at a pre-olympic junior meet for the communist bloc countries. In 1973 and 1974, she was declared an all-around junior champion.

As she grew up, Nadia started to participate in senior level competitions. She got international fame at the European Championships in 1975. She won the gold medal in every routine, beating five-time European champion Turishcheva, except in the floor exercises, in which she scored silver.

The next year was a turning point in her gymnastics career. Comăneci started the year by winning the 1976 American Cup. She was the first woman to perform a backward double salto while dismounting from the uneven parallel bars. Comăneci again created history at the 1976 Olympic Games in Montreal. She was rewarded with seven perfect scores and three gold medals for the balance beam, the uneven bars and individual all-around. At the age of fourteen, she was recognized as the youngest woman to score a perfect ten in an Olympic gymnastics event. Nadia will always remain the youngest gymnast to hold this record because the Olympics age-eligibility requirements were increased to sixteen years.

In 1977, Comăneci earned her second European world title. However, her performance started getting affected when she found out about her parents' divorce. There were also other troubles, because the Romanian sports officials had forcibly changed her coach, whom she eventually got reinstated. As a result, Comăneci didn't perform well at the 1978 World Championships, finishing in fourth place.

She came back in form in 1979 and claimed her third European all-around title. Nadia was the first gymnast to have achieved three all-around titles. Despite an infected hand and hospitalization for blood poisoning, Comăneci persevered. She scored 9.95 for her routine and won her team the gold medal, a first for Romania.

In 1980, Nadia made her return to the Summer Olympics in Moscow. She won two gold and one silver medal in that season. In 1981, she was invited to participate in the United States official tour which was named "Nadia '81". The same year, coach Karolyi defected to the United States while touring. This affected Nadia's career. In 1984, she retired from competing.

In 1989, she left her country and moved to the United States and in 2001 Comăneci officially became a US citizen. Apart from her gymnastics career, she did some modeling projects and starred in a few advertisements.

Nadia, as a former gymnast, was known for her clean routines and using complex skills in competitions. Till date, she is given credit for the specific techniques that she first introduced in her routines. She was the first gymnast to successfully perform an aerial walkover and an aerial cartwheel–back flight series. Apart from her innovative routines, the music that she used in the 1976 Olympics became famous all over the world. It was referred to as "Nadia's Theme". The musical score was later used in many films and theatre. In 1993, Comăneci became the second person to be inducted into the International Gymnastics Hall of Fame. Nadia was also a great writer and released her book titled *Letters to a Young Gymnast* in 2003.

Nadia married American gymnast Bart Conner in 1996. The couple gave birth to their only son in 2006. Nadia and her husband support and help the underprivileged. They founded the Nadia Comăneci Gymnastics School and also opened Nadia Children's Clinic to provide free and low-cost medical and social aid to Romanian kids. Nadia owns a magazine called the *International Gymnast* and a television production company, Perfect 10 Productions, Inc., with her husband.

P. V. SINDHU

BIRTH: July 5, 1995
Hyderabad, India

P. V. Sindhu is an Indian badminton player who is the first Indian woman to win a silver medal at the Olympics.

P. V. Sindhu was born as Pusarla Venkata Sindhu on July 5, 1995, in Hyderabad, India, to P. V. Ramana and P. Vijaya. Both her parents were national level volleyball players. Her father was a recipient of the Arjuna Award in 2000. Even though her parents were former professional volleyball players, Sindhu chose to play badminton. She was inspired by Pullela Gopichand's success at the All England Open Badminton Championship in 2001.

Sindhu started playing badminton at the age of eight. She used to practice under the famous badminton coach, Mehboob Ali. She later joined Pullela Gopichand's badminton academy to further improve her badminton skills. After joining the academy, Sindhu was molded into a professional player.

Sindhu won many titles under the coaching of Pullela Gopichand. She started her career early by winning the doubles title at the 5th Servo All India Championship in the under-10 category. In the same category, she won the singles title at the Ambuja Cement All India tournament. She won the doubles title at the Sub-juniors Nationals, and the All India Ranking in Pune in the under-13 category. She went on to participate in the under-14 category and won a gold medal in the 51st National School Games in India.

Sindhu started her professional badminton career and made her international debut in 2009. She won a bronze medal in the Sub-Junior Asian Badminton Championship. In 2010, she claimed the silver medal in the women's singles at Iran Fajr

International Badminton Challenge. The same year she reached the quarterfinals of the Junior World Badminton Championships in Mexico.

Sindhu entered the 2012 Li Ning China Masters Super Series finals and amazed everyone by defeating the 2012 Olympic gold medalist, Li Xuerui. However, she lost in the semifinals to Jiang Yanjiao. After a good performance in the China Open, her streak faltered in the Japan Open due to a knee injury she'd sustained earlier.

Unaware of her injury at the time, Sindhu participated in the 77th Senior National Badminton Championships in Srinagar in 2012. She was defeated in the finals by Sayali Gokhale. After the championship, she took several weeks to recover from her injury and return to her form.

Sindhu made her grand comeback in 2013 and won her first Grand Prix title in the Malaysia Open. The same year she became India's first medalist in the women's singles at the Badminton World Championships. She ended the year on a bright note by winning the Macau Open Grand Prix Gold title. At the age of eighteen, she received the highest honor for sportspersons in India, the Arjuna Award.

In 2014, Sindhu became the first ever Indian in history to win back-to-back medals in the BFW World Badminton Championship. In 2015, she reached the finals of the Denmark Open by defeating three seeded players. The same year she gained victory for the second time at the Macau Open Grand Prix Gold championship in the women's singles division. In 2016, Sindhu made history by reaching the semifinal of the women's singles event at the 2016 Summer Olympics in Rio. Sindhu competed with Carolina Marin in the finals, winning the first set but losing the other two. Even though she lost the game, she made her country proud and became the first and youngest Indian woman, at the age of 21, to win an Olympic silver medal.

In 2017, she won the India Open Superseries title against Carolina Marin.

For her great contribution to the field of sports, Sindhu has received many awards and honors. She got the FICCI Breakthrough Sportsperson of the Year Award in 2014. NDTV also named her 'Sportsperson of the Year'. She received the Padma Shri Award, the fourth highest civilian honor in India, in 2015. She even received the most significant award for an athlete in India, the Rajiv Gandhi Khel Ratna Award, in 2016.

Despite hectic schedules and training, she started working at Bharat Petroleum company as an assistant sports manager in July 2013. After her win at the Rio Olympics, Sindhu was promoted to the post of deputy sports manager.

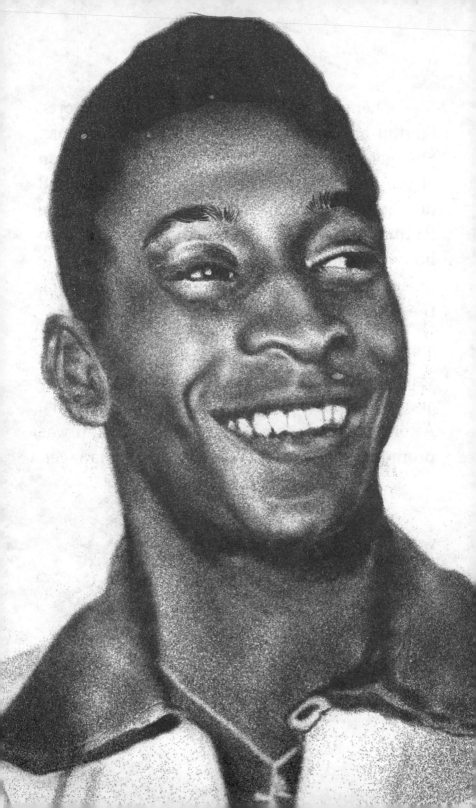

PELÉ

BIRTH: October 23, 1940
Três Corações, Brazil

Pelé is a Brazilian soccer player considered to be the greatest player of all time. He was a member of the Brazilian team that won three World Cups, in 1958, 1962, and 1970. Pelé was called the "King of Football", and he was the highest-paid athlete in the world during his time.

Pelé was born as Edson Arantes do Nascimento on October 23, 1940, in Brazil to João Ramos and Dona Celeste Arantes. He is the elder of two siblings. His parents named him after the American inventor Thomas Alva Edison. He got his nickname Pelé from his friends when he was in school. Edson once mispronounced the goalkeeper Bilé's name as Pelé and it stuck.

Pelé grew up in a low-income environment. From a very young age, Pelé had to start doing odd jobs to earn money and support his family. His father was a former soccer player, which nurtured his interest in the sport. He was the one who taught Pelé to play football. Sometimes Pelé would practice by filling socks with rags because he could not afford a real ball.

Pelé soon started training under Waldemar de Brito, a former member of the Brazilian national soccer team. His coach recognized his talent and wanted him to participate in the Santos professional soccer club. At the age of fifteen, he left his home and tried out for Santos Football Club, he signed a contract with the club in 1956. Pelé played his first professional game that year. At the age of sixteen, he secured the first professional goal of his career. By 1957, he was a permanent player in the team. Soon he was also the top scorer in the league. This performance of his landed him in the national team of Brazil.

In 1957, Pelé played his first international game, against Argentina. Even though his team didn't win, Pelé became the youngest player ever to score a goal in an international soccer tournament. The year 1958 was the turning point in Pelé's career. In 1958, he participated in his first World Cup in Sweden. He made history by breaking several records. He scored a total of six goals in four games that season, making Brazil the winning team of the year. Pelé also helped his team win the Campeonato Paulista league, a top-tier professional soccer league in Brazil. He was the top scorer with 58 goals, which is a record in itself and remains unbroken.

In 1962, Pelé took part in the second World Cup tournament. Due to severe injuries he had to leave the tournament after two games; but Brazil went on to win the World Cup for the second time. That year, Santos FC participated in and won the Copa Libertadores competition, Campeonato Brasiliero and the 1962 Intercontinental Cup. Pelé's most significant career moment came in 1969 when he scored his 1000th goal during the

US League against Vasco da Gama. The goal was dubbed as "The Thousandth".

1970 was another major year for Pelé as he participated in his last World Cup. Brazil won the World Cup in Mexico, and Pelé was applauded for his outstanding performance including a goal in the finals. In 1974, Pelé announced his retirement. The 1974 season with Santos was his nineteenth and final season with the team.

In 1975, he signed a $7 million contract with the New York Cosmos and played with them for a short while. Pelé helped the club to win the 1977 NASL championship and officially retired from soccer.

Pelé has received many prestigious awards and honors in his life, and not just for sports. In 1978, he received the International Peace Award for his work with UNICEF. He worked as a UN Goodwill Ambassador for the Earth Summit in 1992. In 1995, he was named as a UNESCO Goodwill Ambassador and he received Brazil's gold medal for his contribution to sports, and humanitarian and environmental problems. In 1997, he was honored as a Knight Commander of the Order of the British Empire. In 2005, he received the BBC Sports Personality of the Year Lifetime Achievement Award.

Pelé has been married and divorced twice, and is currently married, for a third time, to Marcia Aoki with whom he tied the knot in 2016. He is the father of 7 children.

The term "The Beautiful Game", a synonym for soccer, was popularized by Pelé. While the actual origin of the phrase is unknown, Pelé used this phrase in his 1977 autobiography *My Life and the Beautiful Game*, and it caught on. People called him "The Black Pearl", "The King of Football" and simply "The King".

ROGER
FEDERER

BIRTH: August 8, 1981
Basel, Switzerland

Roger Federer is a Swiss tennis player recognized as one of the greatest tennis players of the 21st century. Federer remained on the world number one spot for a record of 302 weeks overall. He is famously known as "Fed Express". People even call him "Maestro" for his excellent skills.

Roger Federer was born on August 8, 1981, in Basel, Switzerland to Robert Federer and Lynette Federer. He took up tennis and soccer at the age of eight.

By the time Roger turned eleven, he was already amongst the Top 3 Junior Tennis Players in Switzerland. At the age of fourteen, he started to receive tennis coaching. His hard work and hours of practice secured him the title of the national junior champion in Switzerland when he was fourteen. This earned him a sponsorship at the Swiss National Tennis Center in Ecublens.

In 1996, Roger was selected as a member of the International Tennis Federation Junior Tennis Circle and got his first sponsorship at sixteen. He won the junior Wimbledon title and the Orange Bowl in 1998, shortly before he turned professional. He was known as the ITF World Junior Tennis Champion of the Year.

Roger's first professional match was against Lucas Arnold Ker in Switzerland, which he lost. Finally, in 2001, he won the Hopman Cup. The same year he won his first singles title at the Milan Indoor Tournament. In 2001, he became the talk of the town after defeating reigning singles champion Pete Sampras, in the 2001 Wimbledon. He entered the top ten tennis rankings for the first time after winning the Master Series at the Hamburg Masters.

In the year 2003, Federer finally got his first win at the Wimbledon singles. He was the first Swiss man to win the Grand Slam title. Following his victory, Federer held the number three spot in the world rankings. In 2004, he got three singles titles, in the Australian Open, Wimbledon and the US Open. His back-to-back victories placed him at world number one ranking. He continued to win titles and retained his No. 1 ranking from 2004 to 2008.

Federer was the first player to reach the finals of four matches in one calendar year. He won the 2007 Australian Open, his tenth Grand Slam title. He became the second male player, in more than a hundred years, to earn five consecutive Wimbledon titles. Federer stayed at the No. 1 rank for 52 weeks. By 2009, he was considered as the "greatest player in tennis history" by tennis critics and his peers. In June 2009, Federer won his first French Open, his fourteenth Grand Slam title.

However, Federer's performance was rocky in 2010. Federer started the year by winning the

Australian Open. But he failed to reach the semi-finals of the French Open and Wimbledon. His ranking slipped to the number two spot. It was the first time since 2002 that Federer hadn't won the Grand Slam.

In 2011, in a global study, Federer was voted as the second most respected, admired and trusted person in the world, after Nelson Mandela. But he had a relatively slow year, failing to win the Grand Slam once again. In 2012 he finally won the Wimbledon by defeating Andy Murray, winning his seventh title for the championship. In the 2012 Summer Olympics he won a silver medal, and a gold in the doubles. In 2013, he started to get coached by Severin Luthi and Stefan Edberg.

In 2015, Federer had the honor of being the third man in the open era with more than a thousand wins. Federer also won the Gerry Weber Open nine times. Federer passed the fourth round of the 2016 Australian Open and became the first male player to win 300 Grand Slam singles matches. But his form suffered a lot in 2016. He sustained a knee injury and underwent surgery to repair a torn muscle in his knee. In 2017, Federer defeated his rival Rafael Nadal in the final of the Australian Open, winning his record-breaking eighteenth Grand Slam title.

Aside from his incredible sportsmanship, Federer does a lot of charitable work. In 2003, he founded the Roger Federer Foundation to help disadvantaged children with their education. Federer is a member of the South African-Swiss charity called IMBEWU.

Federer married Mirka Vavrinec, a former Women's Tennis Association player on April 11, 2009. They first met during the Sydney Olympics in 2000. The tennis couple are parents to twin daughters and twin sons.

SACHIN TENDULKAR

BIRTH: *April 24, 1973*
Mumbai, India

Sachin Tendulkar is a retired Indian cricketer known to be one of the greatest sports personalities of his generation. He is called the "Milestone Man" in international cricket history.

Sachin Ramesh Tendulkar was born on April 24, 1973, in Mumbai, India to Ramesh and Rajni Tendulkar. Sachin's older brother was the one who encouraged him to play cricket. He was first enrolled at the cricket academy under the coach Ramakant Achrekar. For his studies, Sachin went to Sharadashram Vidyamandir High School. He was part of the school's cricket team and shone as a star cricketer from a very young age. In 1988, he and his friend Vinod Kambli made a record in an interschool match against St Xavier's High School. He managed to score 329 out of a world-record partnership of 664 runs in a school match.

In the same year, Sachin began his domestic career, playing for Mumbai against Gujarat. In his very first match, Sachin scored a century and finished the season as the highest run scorer. Despite having played only in one season, he landed on the national team. In 1989, he made his international debut against Pakistan. With his dedication to the sport, he soon made his debut in the One Day International (ODI) format of the game.

From 1991–92 Tendulkar toured Australia and scored a couple of centuries (148 in Sydney, 114 in Perth). In 1994, he scored his first ODI century against Australia in Sri Lanka.

Sachin was also made captain of the Indian cricket team twice, but both times the results were unexpected. In 1996, he succeeded Azharuddin as captain, however, due to his poor win percentage of 16%, he gave up the captaincy temporarily. In his next captaincy, he obtained a slightly better, but still disappointing, win percentage of 31% and gave up captaincy altogether.

In 2003, India played in the World Cup. Tendulkar gave a remarkable performance on the field and made around 600 runs in eleven matches, averaging a score of 60.2. His hard work paid off and helped India to reach the finals. Although India lost in the finals to Australia, Sachin was awarded as the "Man of the Tournament". In 2005, Tendulkar scored his record-breaking 35th century in a test match against Sri Lanka. For the next couple of years he went through a difficult phase, but in 2007, he was once again in full form. That year he became the first player ever to score 15,000 runs in the ODIs.

In 2011, Tendulkar played against South Africa in the World Cup, during which he scored two centuries. In the finals, India faced Sri Lanka and won the match. For Tendulkar, it was his first World Cup victory. In 2013, he announced his retirement from all forms of cricket.

Tendulkar has won many awards and has many achievements under his belt. As one of the most prolific cricketers in the world, he was the first person to score a double century in the ODIs. In 2012, he became the first cricketer to score 100 centuries in international play. In all forms of international cricket, he scored over 30,000 runs. He is still revered among his fans in cricket-crazy India. Sachin Tendulkar holds the world record for highest number of runs and centuries in both, test cricket matches and the One Day Internationals.

For his exceptional cricket career, Tendulkar received several awards from the Government of India. For his 1997–98 season, he was awarded India's highest sporting award, Rajiv Gandhi Khel Ratna in 1998. He also received India's highest civilian honor, the Bharat Ratna in 2014. He was the first sportsperson to win this award.

Tendulkar also dedicates his time and efforts to charities like Apnalaya, an NGO that sponsors 200 underprivileged children every year for free education, stationery and uniforms. The proceeds from the sales of his book *Playing it My Way*, were forwarded to help fight child malnutrition. He used his status to raise large amounts of funds for cancer research, education and other noble causes.

In 1990, Sachin met Anjali Mehta, a pediatrician, and the couple got married in 1995. They have two children. His son Arjun is now a budding cricketer.

SERENA WILLIAMS

BIRTH: September 26, 1981
Saginaw, Michigan, USA

Serena Williams is the most famous American professional tennis player in the history of the game. Serena has won 23 Grand Slam singles titles in her career, more than any other tennis player during the open era.

Serena Williams was born as Serena Jameka Williams on September 26, 1981, in Saginaw, Michigan, to Oracene Price and Richard Williams. Serena started to take an interest in tennis at the age of three. Her father says that she played her first tournament at the age of four and a half and went on to win all but three tournaments in the next five years.

In 1991, Serena was ranked number one in the under-10 category. By the age of fourteen, Serena had already turned professional. But the Women's Tennis Association felt she was too young and thus barred her from competing in WTA events. So, she played her first match as a professional in 1995 at Quebec, Canada in a non-WTA event.

In 1998, Williams made her professional debut in her first Grand Slam tournament at the Australian Open. In 1999, she played the French Open and the US Open with her sister Venus Williams. The sisters won the doubles. Moreover, Serena won the finals of the US Open Grand Slam singles tournament. Serena became the second African-American woman ever to have accomplished this feat. Serena reached the world number four position in the second year of her professional career.

In 2000, Serena teamed up with her sister

Venus once again and won a gold medal at the Sydney Olympics. The sisters also got their first Wimbledon title. In 2001, the Williams sisters won the doubles title at the Australian Open. The sisters were the first in history to win all four Grand Slam women's doubles titles.

The year 2002 was the best year for Serena's career. She won the French Open, the Wimbledon and the US Open, all against her sister in the finals. Serena was the first African-American to end the season at the number one world ranking. Her accomplishments didn't stop there. In 2003, she won the Australian Open, against her sister once again, and became the fifth female tennis player to win all four major titles simultaneously. This feat was dubbed as a "Serena Slam" by the media. With all the record-breaking matches, she started to experience burnout and her health began to suffer. In 2003, Serena underwent knee surgery and it took months for her to recover.

Serena made her comeback at the 2007 Australian Open. She defeated the famous tennis player Maria Sharapova and won her third

Australian Open title. In 2008, Serena and her sister Venus teamed up to win the women's doubles title at Wimbledon and their second doubles gold medal at the 2008 Olympics. In 2009, Serena climbed back to the number one world rank for the second time in her career. She achieved her tenth Grand Slam title by winning the Australian Open that year.

Serena made history by winning the singles gold medal at the 2012 Olympics, becoming the second woman to win a career Golden Slam. She also won her fifteenth Grand Slam singles title the same year at the US Open. She won the Rogers Cup, the China Cup and WTA championships. By 2016, Serena had been at the world number one spot for 157 consecutive weeks.

After losing several matches in 2016, Serena started 2017 on a promising note. She won the Australian Open against her sister Venus. It was the 23rd Grand Slam singles title of her career. Later she announced her pregnancy and revealed that she was eight-weeks pregnant during the game. She gave birth to a baby girl in September 2017.

The same year she married her long-time fiancé, and Reddit founder, Alexis Ohanian.

Apart from her tennis career, Serena also grew her brand power through films, television and fashion. She was a voice actor in a couple of television shows like *The Simpsons* and also appeared on the covers of famous magazines. In 2004, Serena launched her design label, Aneres. Serena was the first black female athlete to appear on *Vogue*'s cover in 2015. The Williams sisters also published a couple of books. Serena's first book was called *Venus & Serena: Serving from the Hip: 10 Rules for Living, Loving and Winning*. In 2009, Serena released her autobiography called *On the Line*.

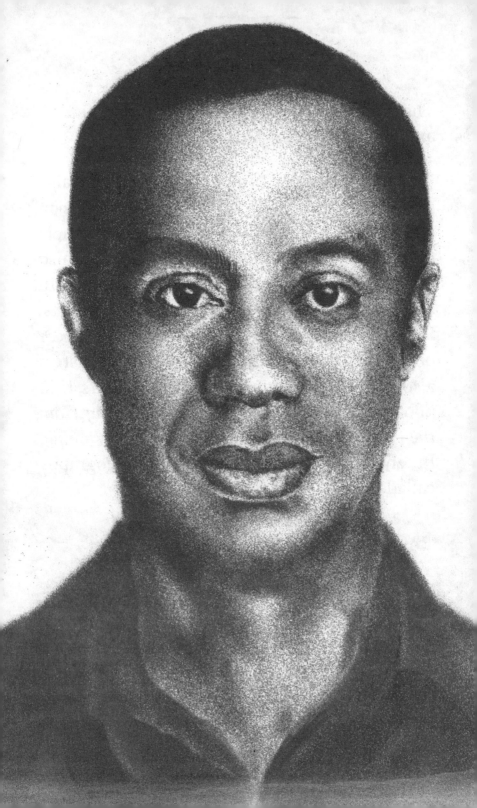

TIGER WOODS

BIRTH: December 30, 1975
Cypress, California, USA

Tiger Woods is an American professional golfer and one of the highest-paid athletes in the world. He was the first and youngest African American to win the US Masters in 1997.

Tiger Woods, also known as Eldrick Tont Woods was born on December 30, 1975, in Cypress, California to Earl Woods and Kultida. His father started calling Eldrick "Tiger" in honor of a fellow soldier. Tiger was inclined towards golf from a very young age. He started playing when he was only two years old.

When Woods was four, his parents hired a coach for him. At the age of six, he began to participate in junior contests. Tiger won the under-10 competition at the Navy Golf Course, Cypress. From 1988 to 1991 he took part in many Junior World Golf Championships. Woods won the tournament six times. In 1991, at the age of fifteen, Woods became the youngest champion of the US Junior Amateur championship.

Woods started his professional career in 1996. He immediately signed advertising deals with Nike and Titleist due to his booming success during his college days. In 1997, he made history by winning his first major competition, the Masters Tournament. He became the tournament's youngest-ever winner at the age of 21. In just two months he was the number one player in the world. This was the fastest any golfer had reached that spot in their career. In 1999, he won the PGA Championship. In the following years he was either winning or finishing in the top ten positions of every match he participated in.

In the year 2000, at the age of 24, Woods won four major golf tournaments: the US Open, US

Amateur, the British Open and British Amateur Championship. He started the new millennium at the top of his career. He achieved six back-to-back wins, the longest winning streak since 1948. Woods became the youngest athlete to achieve the Career Grand Slam. He had won nine PGA tournaments by then. In 2001, Woods won the Masters Tournament. He was the first player to win all four major professional titles at the same time.

The 2003–2004 season was not a great one for Woods' career. He didn't win any major games in these two years and thus lost his number one ranking. In 2005, Woods returned to his form. He won two majors and rose to the top of the rankings. The next two years, Woods continued his streak and closed the 2006 season with 54 wins, including the PGA Championship and the British Open.

In 2008, Woods suffered from episodic pain in his left knee due to an arthroscopic surgery from earlier that year. Woods had to take a short break from golfing and missed the rest of the PGA tour season. He returned to the game in

2009 but the season didn't pan out as planned. He didn't win a single major event, even losing the PGA title, although he did remain at the number one spot in the world rankings. The year also brought some personal misfortune for Woods. He was involved in a car accident one early morning in November which led to the revelation of his multiple extra-marital affairs. Following this event, many sponsors canceled his contracts, and his ranking naturally dropped.

Woods took an indefinite leave from golfing to spend more time with his family. He made his comeback in 2010 but it was a disappointing season with no tournament wins. The 2012 season was much better for him. He won two tournaments, the Arnold Palmer Invitational and the Memorial Tournament. In 2013, he won the Farmers Insurance Open and WGC Cadillac Championship. He won the Arnold Palmer Invitational for the eighth time and shot to the top of the world rankings.

In 2014, Woods started to experience incessant back pain. He underwent back surgery and struggled well into 2016 to return to the game, missing the entire season. He made a comeback in 2017 that didn't last long due to another back surgery. He finally won a Tour Championship in September 2018, his first victory in five years.

Woods rose to extraordinary heights with his sheer dedication and hard work. He has been recognized as the "greatest closer in history" with 79 official PGA Tour events victories. He was the youngest among the few players to have won all four professional major championships, achieving a career Grand Slam.

He is also the only one to win all 4 four, in a row, this unique achievement came to be known as a 'Tiger Slam'. Woods was inducted to the California Museum for History, Women and the Arts in Sacramento in 2007. *The Associated Press* described him as "Athlete of the Decade" in 2009.

Woods married Elin Nordegren in 2004, with whom he has two children. However, the couple got divorced in 2010.

USAIN BOLT

BIRTH: August 21, 1986
Montego Bay, Jamaica

Usain Bolt is a Jamaican sprinter and Olympic legend. He is recognized as "the fastest man alive". He achieved the "triple triple", winning three gold medals in three consecutive Olympic Games, making a total of nine.

Usain Bolt was born as Usain St Leo Bolt on August 21, 1986 in Sherwood Content, Jamaica to Jennifer and Wellesley Bolt. As a kid, Bolt used to spend his time playing cricket and football with his brother. Bolt had always been a fast runner and participated in many school competitions. He won many 10-meter running games in school. After completing his primary education, he moved to the William Knibb Memorial High School. Bolt had an interest in every sport. But his cricket coach noticed Bolt's speed on the field and encouraged him to try track and field. Bolt started to get trained by a former Olympic sprinter named Pablo McNeil.

At the age of fourteen, Usain participated in his first high school championship. He won silver in the 200-meter race with his lightning speed. In 2001, he participated in the first major international sporting event called the IAAF World Youth Championship. Even though Bolt didn't win the 200-meter race, he finished the race in 21.73 seconds. It was his personal best at the time. By the time he was fifteen, he had grown to 6 ft. 5 inches in height and already stood out amongst his rivals.

In 2002, Bolt participated in the World Junior Championships. He won the gold medal in the 200 meters race, making him the youngest junior gold medalist in the world. In 2003, Bolt participated in the Jamaican High School Championships. He won both, the 200-meter and 400-meter running events in record time. The same year he won gold at the World Youth Championship.

Bolt started his professional career in 2004 under coach fitz Coleman. That year, he participated in three events, the 2004 CARIFTA Games in Bermuda, the 2004 World Junior Championships and the popular 2004 Athens Olympics. However, he failed the 200-meter Olympic qualifier event due to a leg injury.

In 2005, Bolt started to train with a new coach named Glen Mills. Bolt finished his next 200-meter race in just 19.99 seconds. He entered the world Top 5 rankings in 2005 and 2006. In 2006, Bolt sustained a severe injury and couldn't participate in the 2006 Commonwealth Games. The only event he won was the IAAF World Athletics Final in Germany. Unfortunately, his injuries continued to trouble him. It limited him from completing a full professional season. In 2007, Bolt made his comeback by participating in the IAAF World T&F Championships, earning two silver medals and breaking the 200-meter record.

Bolt showed his full potential in 2008 when he participated in his first Olympics. He won three gold medals in the 100-meter, 200-meter, and 400-meter relay. He set new world records in all three events and became an icon. In 2009, Bolt participated in the Berlin World Championships. He once again broke his previous world records in the 100-meter and 200-meter races. He finished the 100-meter race in 9.58 seconds.

In 2016, Bolt achieved the "triple-triple" after participating in the Rio Olympics. He won three gold medals in three consecutive Olympic games.

2017 was the worst year of Bolt's career. He didn't perform well in any of his matches, and many believed that the 400-meter relay would be Bolt's final race. During the race Bolt fell and sustained a hamstring injury. He had to cross the finish line with the help of his teammates.

The same year Bolt announced his retirement from track and field.

Apart from his sport, Bolt is involved in a lot of humanitarian work. He donated $50,000 to the victims of the 2008 Siachen earthquake. He started the Usain Bolt Foundation, dedicated to providing educational and cultural development for disadvantaged children.

Bolt has always remained private about his relationships. Currently, he is in a relationship with Jamaican model Kasi Bennett. They recently made their relationship public.

WAYNE GRETZKY

BIRTH: January 26, 1961
Brantford, Canada

Wayne Gretzky is a Canadian-born former ice hockey player. He is called "the Great One" in the world of ice hockey. He made 61 NHL records by the time he retired in 1999.

Wayne Gretzky was born as Wayne Douglas Gretzky on January 26, 1961 in Ontario, Canada to Walter Gretzky and Phyllis Gretzky. Wayne was only two when he held a hockey stick for the first time at his grandfather's house.

Wayne's father was his first coach, who taught him the basics of hockey. By the time he was six, his father had built him a rink in the family's backyard. He started to skate there for hours every day. Wayne learned everything about the game without any professional coaching. Later he was trained by Dick Martin. His coach described Wayne as a child prodigy. Wayne played in many leagues above his age; the other players in his team were four years senior to him. In his junior seasons, he'd amassed 378 goals.

In 1977, Wayne was the third player to be drafted in the Ontario Major Junior Hockey League Midget draft for Sault Ste. Marie Greyhounds. In 1978, he experienced his first international success. He was selected for the 1978 World Junior Championships in Quebec. The next year Wayne played a full season in the OHA, finishing second, and wore his iconic No. 99 shirt for the first time.

In 1979, Gretzky played for the first time in an NHL season despite his young age. For his outstanding performance that season he received the Hart Memorial Trophy as the 'Most Valuable

Player' in the league. Gretzky became the first ever first-year player to receive this award. In the 1981–82 season, he scored a record of 92 goals. He was the first person to break the 200-point limit in one season with 212 points. That season Gretzky earned seven scoring titles.

Gretzky played for many years for the Edmon-ton Oilers. He helped his team to win the Stanley Cup four times, in 1984, 1985, 1987 and 1988. The year 1987 was the most significant one. Gretzky ended the season with 52 goals and 163 assists, which naturally made him one of the best hockey players of all time. The Canadian government honored Gretzky with a Wayne Gretzky Dollar Coin, which is among the highest Canadian civilian honors.

In 1988, the Oilers traded Gretzky to the LA Kings team for some money and players. It was the biggest deal in the history of hockey. In 1988 Gretzky played for his team for the last time. Many fans were angry about Gretzky's decision to leave for the United States.

At the end of 1988, Gretzky played for the LA Kings for the first time. He played with them for eight seasons and led his team to many victories. In 1993, his team reached the Stanley Cup finals, however they lost the game to the Montreal Canadians. Gretzky won four more Hart and Art Ross trophies and broke many records.

In 1996, Gretzky joined the St Louis Blues team for a short while. He played only one season with them. Next year he joined the New York Rangers hockey team. He was a part of the team for three hockey seasons. In 1977, his team reached the Eastern Conference Finals but lost the game to the Philadelphia Flyers. In 1999, he broke another record by scoring a total of 1071 goals in all his games. The same year, Gretzky announced his retirement.

Gretzky's jersey number 99 has been retired league-wide. He is the first hockey player whose jersey number was taken out of circulation by a team as a way of honoring a former player. Gretzky was inducted to the Hockey Hall of Fame in 1999. He has earned 61 NHL records, has the most career goals (894), and the most career points (2,857). Throughout his career in hockey, he was awarded with ten Art Ross Memorial Trophies, nine Hart Trophies and five Ted Lindsay awards. Many awards in sports have been named in his honor.

After his retirement, Gretzky became a hockey coach. He became a minority owner of the Phoenix Coyotes in 2000 and was named their head coach in 2005 until 2009. He also opened his own restaurant business and wine business in California. Wayne did various TV shows during his active years. He was a judge on the *Dance Fever* show and has also done talk shows over the years. During the show *Dance Fever* he met his future wife, Janet Jones. They got married in 1988 and have five children.

QUESTIONS

Q.1. Which club was Ronaldo playing for before he joined Manchester United?

Q.2. Against which team did Ronaldo score his first goal for Manchester United?

Q.3. When was David Beckham born?

Q.4. After the 1936 Olympics, what role did Jesse Owens undertake?

Q.5. Which team did LeBron James play for in 2003?

Q.6. Maradona has played for two Spanish clubs. The first one was Barcelona, which was the other one?

Q.7. Which high school did LeBron James go to?

Q.8. How old was Lionel Messi when he made his Barcelona debut?

Q.9. How many gold medals did Jesse Owens win at the 1936 Olympics?

Q.10. What position did David Beckham play in

the squad?

Q.11. What was the name of the high school that Michael Jordan attended?

Q.12. When was Mary Kom born and what sport does she play?

Q.13. Which country did Michael Phelps swim for?

Q.14. Who was Mary Kom's first coach?

Q.15. How old was Nadia Comăneci when she scored perfect 10s in the Montreal Olympics?

Q.16. In which year was Sachin Tendulkar awarded the Bharat Ratna?

Q.17. Where did Serena Williams play her first WTA match?

Q.18. What sport did Michael Jordan play professionally?

Q.19. Apart from her sister Venus, who is the only other player that Serena Williams has won a Grand Slam doubles title with?

Q.20. Where did Roger Federer win his first Grand Slam?

Q.21. What was Pelé's first job?

Q.22. Who was Nadia Comăneci's coach?

Q.23. Where on August 16, 2009, did Usain set a world record for the 100-meter and 200-meter races?

Q.24. When was Sachin Tendulkar born and what are the names of his parents?

Q.25. Which CFL team did Wayne partly own with former LA Kings owner Bruce McNall and the late John Candy?

Q.26. Usain Bolt belonged to which 2010 athletics club based in Kingston?

Q.27. Who was Ali's opponent in "The Rumble in the Jungle"?

Q.28. Who was Wayne's favorite player when he was growing up?

Q.29. In which tournament did Maria Sharapova win her first match?

Q.30. Which city hosted the Olympics when Muhammad Ali won his gold medal?

DID YOU KNOW?

1. Ronaldo has scored 99 doubles throughout his career. 73 with Real Madrid, 25 with Manchester United and one with Sporting Portugal.

2. Michael Jordan starred in the 1996 feature film *Space Jam*, portraying himself.

3. David Beckham is the first English player to win league titles in four countries, i.e. England, Spain, the United States and France.

4. At the age of nine, Nadia became the youngest gymnast ever to win the Romanian nationals.

5. After he retired, Michael Jordan joined the Washington Wizards as a part owner and president of basketball operations.

6. David Beckham was inducted into the English Football Hall of Fame in 2008.

7. In the 2014–15 season, Beckham scored nineteen goals in ten consecutive games. It was a record for a Real Madrid player.

8. Mary Kom is a five-time AIBA champion in

senior boxing.

9. P. V. Sindhu was awarded the Padma Shri, the highest civilian award of India in the year 2015.

10. Nadia Comăneci is the first gymnast to be awarded a perfect score of ten in the Olympics.

11. Jesse Owens worked in a shoe repair shop after school and found his passion for running at that time.

12. Diego Maradona made his international debut for Argentina, against Hungary in 1977, when he was sixteen years old.

13. Diego Maradona could not make it to the team in the 1978 World Cup. He was considered too young at the age of seventeen by coach Cesar Luis Menotti.